MY MILLIONAIRE KIDS

The true story of how two ordinary kids are on their way to become millionaires and how to make your child a Millionaire

I0161015

By

Lyn DeVincenzo

Presents:

The MMK System

My Millionaire Kids: The MMK System

ISBN : 978-0-9831040-0-1

Copyright 2012   By Kathlyn G. DeVincenzo
3208C E. Colonial Dr. Ste 286
Orlando, Florida 32803

Published by My Millionaire Kids, LLC
3208C E. Colonial Dr. Ste. 286
Orlando, Florida 32803
Lyn@mmksystem.com
407-766-1925

DEDICATION

Dedicated to my parents. I owe my success, happiness and who I am more to you than to anyone or anything else. You pointed me in the right direction - because you were going that way. You gave me a good foundation of discipline, hard work and honesty.

You did a good job without much help. I hope this book makes it easier for all the people trying to do a good job of parenting today.

TABLE OF CONTENTS

Preface

It took me several years to realize that the success of my children was actually due to actions that I had taken as a parent starting at a very young age. At some point I realized their accomplishments were not about natural talent, but there were certain critically important life skills I had taught Matthew and Milena that had given them an advantage. I was surprised to discover that not many other parents were doing this.

I am writing this book because it has been proven that other parents can prepare their children for success by applying the same techniques. I have left out all the mistakes and missteps and arranged what I did into a well-organized system. It did not go as smoothly for my family as it can for yours. With the benefit of hindsight, what had been a matter of experimentation has now become a straightforward and effective plan.

If I had to say where everything got started for us, I'd point to a seemingly ordinary night and a comment made by my husband, Ed.

When my son was a baby and we were remodeling our first house, Ed lay in bed exhausted after a long day and announced, "When our son is a teenager, I am going to buy a house and have him remodel it so he won't have any time to get into trouble. "

Ed was joking, but that's exactly what happened. Years later we partnered with him on a house which he remodeled and now he has rental income from that property. Even better, our daughter and her friends are his tenants, so she got to live on her own, but under our watchful eye. How we got from Ed's humorous comment to the reality of Matthew remodeling a home and becoming a landlord is the story behind this book.

Later, when our son was about 6, we were working in the yard and he said, 'I hate yard work."

 I said, "Well, you can scratch "landscape architect" off your list. What do you want to be when you grow up?"

He said, "I want to be a big game hunter in Africa."

To which I replied, "That is not a job, that is an expensive hobby. You had better pick a career that you make a lot of money if you ever want to do that. If you were born in Africa and lived among the animals, you could become a guide and that would be a career, but being born in America, it is not likely you could ever learn to be a guide like the people who are born there."

You will notice, that I did not tell him it was his responsibility to contribute to the family, that we all have to pitch in, etc. While we continued working, I distracted him from his dislike of gardening and used the opportunity to get him thinking about how to find a career he would enjoy.

I also did not say, "You can be anything you want to be." To say this is a great disservice and gives our children false hope and expectations. If you are not tall and agile enough, you cannot be a basketball player. If you don't have a beautiful voice, you can't sing at the Met. We can give our children encouragement and direction without misleading them.

When Matthew said he hated yard work, that was not the same strong emotional statement an adult would make about the misery of his job. It was a mere statement of dislike. Instead of coercing him to work I distracted him a positive way by getting him to talk about what he really wanted to do. Meanwhile we continued to get the yard work done. I gained time for myself by having him share the yard work, and he got to spend time with Mom and develop skills in the bargain.

When our son was in college, he had friends who had a

landscape business and he really enjoyed working with them. Although commercial work is vastly different than our little back yard, the skills he learned as a child made him a valuable employee.

Some skills we learn are specific to a particular job; such as knowing the difference between a weed and a flower. Other skills, such as punctuality, dependability, discipline, self-control apply to all occupations. But all skills create brain paths that are beneficial in work and play. We have heard and understand the term "eye-hand coordination." But we do not realize that learning tasks make our children more effective no matter what their future occupation.

I, too, hated gardening as a child because my mother would send us outside to pull weeds as punishment or to get us out of her hair. I discovered I loved gardening as an adult and now it is one of my favorite activities. I might have enjoyed it more as a child if my mother had worked in the garden with us. We were "in her hair" because we wanted to belong.

When my daughter was 3 and my son 6, I made up a chore chart (Job Description and Schedule). It had 10 things they had to do, for 5 days, and I paid them $.10 per chore. That made their allowance (Wages) $5.00 a week. That sounds like a lot of money for a 3-year old. But at the same time, I transferred some of their purchases to them. If we were out and they wanted to buy a small toy or souvenir, I had them pay for it. I had a great surprise at how quickly they learned the value of a dollar (Cost/Benefit Ratio) and would have bought things if I were paying for it, but not if they were paying for it.

If they didn't do their chores on time, they didn't get paid. If they fought, I took a dime away. I can honestly say I had very little trouble with my children. This system was a very effective form of discipline.

On my chart, they were paid to brush their teeth and go to bed on time. I chose these tasks because they were causing friction in the home. They would hop into bed without brushing their teeth. They would not be ready for school on time. These things may not seem like "chores" but the "Job" of a three-year-old is to take care of herself and her stuff (toys). I never did have to pay them for traditional chores such as washing dishes and doing yard work and I never did have to raise their allowance. By the time they were old enough to help around the house, they understood that we all pitch in and work together.

By age 9 they were self-sufficient, earning all the money they needed outside the home. My daughter started her acting career in commercials and my son started doing yard work and handyman work. Notice that the 6 year old who "hated yard work" was now making his living at it. A small amount of money went a long way because they knew how hard it was to get it.

There is an untold amount of opportunity to earn money. When the neighbors saw my kids working in the yard, they hired them to rake leaves, help clean out the garage and do other menial tasks that adults won't do. They were generous.

I paid other neighborhood kids to work in the yard with me when my kids "graduated" to better jobs.

The work is there, the money is there, the skilled labor pool is lacking. Your kids have jobs waiting for them!

Every two weeks we would go to the bank and deposit their 10% long-term savings. They got a lollipop and praise from the teller. To this day, the ladies at the bank ask about the kids.

I have written the story of my children's success, hoping that it will inspire and motivate you. But this book will be of no benefit to you unless you use the materials at the back of the book and apply the principles to your own lives. Don't delay - get started today.

My Millionaire Kids is a fun title. It's meant to get your attention. But this is not simply a book about making your kids rich or transforming them into skilled workers. Life is about much more than economics. Earning and managing money are an important part of life, but they are not the most important things in life.

The understanding and discipline gained from learning to make and manage money have productive benefits for all areas of life. The money side of things is actually a great by-product. This book is about learning how to make a schedule that matches up with your priorities. It's about harnessing drive and determination toward a goal. It's about character formation. Finally and supremely, it's about family - about relationships and how to care for them. In other words, it's about being a person who is loyal and compassionate toward others, showing respect and consideration. Yet, in order to be that kind of person, you first have to take responsibility for your own life.

Teaching children to take responsibility for their own lives - ultimately as parents, that's what we're trying to do. We are trying to show them how they can mature and become successful adults, living happy, fulfilling, rewarding and secure lives. But this primary endeavor trips up too many parents.

Recently, I surveyed my friends who had children under the age of 12 and asked a very simple question, "What is the number one issue causing frustration in your family?"

The details varied, but the bottom line was, "accept responsibility". One could never find his soccer shoes, several were not on time and prepared to leave the house for school or other activities, others had to be monitored to brush their teeth and most were uncooperative in "doing chores."

Children who are not taught to accept responsibility are not prepared to succeed in the work world in spite of the billions of dollars spent on our educational system and all the additional activities parents pay for out of their own pockets.

As I write this, our economy is going through "The Great Recession." Families are struggling. No one taught us how to properly handle money. No one taught us that economies have cycles and there are going to be bad times. No one taught us that we have to be prepared. Whether our personal situation is down, or the entire economy is down, we should have a cushion. We should have savings. We should have more skills, either to get other jobs or to do more for ourselves. We should have developed the creativity to recognize new opportunities.

We're not well-trained, but we consider ourselves to be responsible adults. Somehow we've managed to accept responsibility and do the best we can holding down a job and a home. But we're stressed out and strapped financially. We're using the same haphazard system our parents used. There isn't enough time to meet obligations and spend time with our children.

My Millionaire Kids allows you to get things done and spend time with your family. It's a system that parents can use even if they weren't well trained as children. These techniques will make your life and your children's lives better. The benefits are now and later. You can learn along with your children. Your home can be the well-run, peaceful, fun place you dreamed of but didn't know how to achieve.

This is a hands-on book that invites participation. My intention is to provide something that can get you started on this wonderful path right away.

The benefits are numerous, but there is one in particular worth emphasizing. *My Millionaire Kids* will allow you to *enjoy* your kids. I put the word "My" in the title to make the point that my kids are still *mine*. They're independent adults now, and we have a great relationship. They tell me what's going on in their lives and still ask for advice, like the rest of my friends.

There's a lot of mutual respect and affection. Such a development was made possible by the things I am going to reveal in this book.

Parents need a system to train their children in such a way that they "accept responsibility" and mature into capable adults. This system should develop them in such a way that they will have the skills, discipline and determination to succeed in good times and bad.

Making matters worse, many parents are already overwhelmed managing their own affairs, and as much as they want the best for their children, the task of learning and implementing something new is faced with exhaustion.

The best thing you can give anyone is time. It's the one thing you never have enough of, the top of everyone's wish list. Even extremely wealthy people frequently complain that they don't have enough time.

By transferring some of the necessary household work to your children in the systematic way I've developed, an exciting method that will cause your children to feel responsible and give them a sense of being important members of the family; you are gaining time to spend with them in enjoyable activities. By taking the stress out of your family, you are creating quality time. That is what this system ensures. *My Millionaire Kids* will assist parents in developing environments of family unity by bringing families together in the pursuit of one of the most worthwhile goals imaginable - making the kind of home in which children feel safe and productive; the kind of home they want when they have families.

That this endeavor will also make children successful achievers in our competitive world is just the icing on the cake. But the icing tastes awfully good.

Chapter 1 "Work is a Four Letter Word"

How can I help my child become one of the people who loves his job? How can I instill a sense of the dignity of work as opposed to work being seen as drudgery?

Almost everyone has to work. Even people who have more than enough money work. Since we spend many, many hours of our lives working, parents wonder how they can turn something that is such a significant aspect of life into a fulfilling adventure.

If so many people are miserable in their jobs, what about the "lucky" people who like their jobs so well that they say, "I would do this for free."

While part of this undeniably has to do with the kind of job a person has, whether his boss is an effective manager or not, and the extent to which a person's job lines up with his talents and desires, there is something else that is very important and often overlooked. The people who are happy at work are usually people who were brought up to see work as a rewarding and exciting component of their lives. It was something they were taught as children.

The way children are taught to work at home and the way they are taught to approach work carries over into their entire lives. Instead of viewing work as a necessary task that is endured for the sake of paying the bills, your children can understand that work is an aspect of a happy and healthy life.

How is this accomplished?

First, children don't naturally have the misconception that work is a source of misery. Before they understand what a job is, what a career is, what it means to make a mortgage payment and purchase groceries, they see themselves within a world that calls out to be explored and conquered. They want to know what makes things tick. *Why? How? Will you show me how to do that? Can I help?* These are the questions that drive parents crazy, and too often we are too busy to give the right answer. This is a huge mistake. These questions reveal that children are by nature curious about the world, and what is more, they desire to know how the world works and *to be a part of its working.*

Children want to build and create. They want to manage and implement an order that is of their own making.

Obviously, that is not *all* children want to do. They also like to tear things up, make clean places dirty, turn procedure into chaos. Every parent is well aware of the wildness within a child. But what is acknowledged less is the flip side of this coin: the wonder and curiosity that children have, the longing to make and to preserve things. These are every bit as strong as the destructive tendencies. Children will wreak havoc on a backyard, "digging a tunnel to China", but if you pay attention, you will also see them trying to lay claim to their surroundings by making some kind of order.

It may be hard to recognize because it is untrained. Ask those poor pet turtles that just want to be free to wander around in their tanks! Children keep trying to make them remain in one part of their habitat, to line them up, to schedule their movements.

Another important truth is that children are natural imitators. First, foremost and lastingly, they imitate their parents. They learn to be a part of this world by doing what their parents do. So how do we as parents take advantage of this insight in a practical way? The way children are taught to work in the home will carry over into their entire work life. *My Millionaire Kids* will show you how to give your children a positive attitude toward work.

 If you weren't given the chance to find your best career and you hate your job, you can prevent your child from ending up in the same boat. Whatever you do, don't make them hate work and don't use it as punishment. They look at work as "something grownups do" and they want to be grown up.

Mom makes her bed - that's a grown up thing, so child wants to do it. Mom cooks - so child wants to do it. Mom gets irritated that the child is following her around. She is under pressure to get too much work done in too little time. Her overworked brain and society's misguided idea that children shouldn't work, block her from teaching that child to make the bed. She is in a hurry just to 'get the job done" so she can go onto another task.

How much better it would be for Mom to take 6 weeks teaching (On the Job Training) the child to make the bed, then after 6 weeks, that is the child's responsibility (Job) and Mom is freed up to do other things. She can even hire the child to make every bed in the home. She invests 6 weeks in training and get about 15 years in return.

In later chapters I will outline in detail how such a transition is possible. We're going to get to how you can put this into practice soon enough. For now, let's look at some words and concepts that are frequently used in the business community and see how they are already a part of your child's mental makeup. These are words and concepts common in the work world.

I have shown that these words describe attributes that are not only about business. They're about being human. And so, they're about children. These words are *hardwired* into us.

1.   Teamwork

We want to feel included. Everyone wants to be a part of something. That is one reason why your child is following you around.

2.   Contribution

People want to feel they are doing something worthwhile. Children have a deep desire to place themselves within what is going on around them and to make their mark. A child of any age can contribute and wants to.

3.   Challenge

People enjoy learning and growing. Children thrive on it and need it. A parent may want to kick back in the recliner, but a child wants to know how the recliner works and to make one from scratch. A child who is bored will either become apathetic or disruptive

4.   Leadership

Wanting to be in control is natural. How many times have you heard a child say to another child, "you ain't da boss o' me!"

The turtle story makes it clear that a child who does not have a younger sibling will boss the pets. Teaching our children to be in control of their environment is giving them skills which prove valuable in the business world. No one likes a boss, but will follow a good leader. We want them to be leaders not bosses. We want them to control their environment, not each other.

5. Skill

Work produces competence. We all learn by doing. In the work world we call this a "Skilled" Employee. Given the traits we've been discussing, it is clear that curiosity and exploration lead to a desire for mastery. The discipline and tenacity required for mastering something require good parenting, but the desire is already there. Skills are the tools of mastery. The higher the skill set, the higher the Compensation, both monetarily and psychologically.

6. Goals

A person who does not feel his life is "getting somewhere" will become depressed. We are designed to achieve success. Children may not communicate that they have goals; they may not know how to reach them, but they have them.

7. Reward

Very few of us can afford to work without a Paycheck. But getting a Paycheck is not a fundamental aspect of being human. It is a particular kind of reward used in a particular kind of society and economy. Long before there were paychecks, there were rewards. Children understand rewards. In addition to our paid work we also volunteer for intangible rewards.

There are more of these terms and concepts, but let's see how to incorporate this into the life of a five-year-old

Mom cooks, cleans, organizes and shops. Dad washes the car, keeps the landscape and keeps the books. These are the things the five-year-old sees. When Mom and/or Dad go to work, the child does not see what they do - they just disappear for a number of hours.

A five-year- old is capable of the following:

1.   Make his bed

2.   Empty the trash cans

3   Put the silverware out

4   Sweep

Let's relate these five tasks that a five-year-old can do to the concepts we've just explored.

1.   Teamwork.

Look at the necessities of life and figure out how to do the work together. For example, Son clears the table, Mom loads the dishwasher, Sister puts the leftovers away and Dad reads the paper.

Another example: Dad mows the lawn, Son clips the hedges, Sister pulls the weeds, and Mom reads a magazine.

Do you see that I have worked some "down time" in here for Mom and Dad? Too many parents do all the work and then try to squeeze "fun" time in with their kids. The "fun" time isn't much fun because Mom and Dad are worn out and no fun. Teamwork gets the work done faster so there is more fun time for all and everyone has energy to enjoy himself.

2.   Contribution

 A child would not put it into words, but there is something missing when Mom and Dad do all the work and the kids are included only in the fun stuff. We are wired to give, as proven by the millions of times kids will go out in the yard, pull up a few weed flowers and proudly bring them in to Mommy; and the drawers full of drawings they have given us over the years.

We continue to Contribute in adulthood as evidence by the many volunteer hours and large sums of money donated to charities.

The above examples under Teamwork, in which even the little five-year-old can participate, also allow for contribution. To be part of a team effort is to make a contribution.

3.   Challenge.

If your child is not challenged he will either be bored or competitive. When my son was 9, he re-grouted one of the bathrooms. He met the challenge and was proud. I had the opportunity to brag on him. He did not have to beat up a neighbor child to prove himself. He did not have to win at something to prove himself. He could be proud of his accomplishment without taking anything away from someone else.

From the perspective of a five-year-old, sweeping or making a bed is a big challenge. If you as a parent frame it correctly, as a part of a Team Effort, everyone has a role to play in making your home a happy one.

4.   Leadership.

A recent article on entrepreneurs stated that (1) they had worked for someone else for many years, (2) they saved their own money to start their business, (3) accounted for over 50% of the GDP and (4) accounted for 75% of job growth in the last 20 years.

Wouldn't it be better to give your child a head start by having him work for "The Family Business" for 20 years, save his own money, discover his own talents, develop his skills and learn business operations, than to have him go out in the workforce in his 20's and start his business in his 40's?

You might think that tasks such as sweeping or making a bed have little to do with leadership. But they are of great significance to a five-year-old. He can see himself as part of a team; as making a contribution and as controlling and leading in his own area of work.

5.   Skills.

When my son remodeled his house, we hired men from the homeless shelter to do demolition and labor. It was heartbreaking for me to see grown men who knew no more about work and had no more skill than a child in kindergarten. One young man in particular had had a run in with drugs and before he went down that slippery slope removed himself from his family environment and voluntarily put himself into a rehab program. He was sweet and polite but went from room to room talking instead of working. I could not keep him on task.

How different his life would have been if his mom had put him to work in The Family Business.

The five-year-old sees everyone in the house doing various jobs, and he has a job to do too. In teaching him to sweep, make the bed and take out the trash, you are developing his practical skills that will grow and expand

6.   Goals.

One of the best ways to avoid wasting money is to have long term goals. Matthew and Milena's first goal was to pay half of their first bike. This kept them from spending their money on every trinket that caught their eye.

7.   Reward.

There are 2 types of reward and we need both: tangible and intangible. In the business world, the tangible reward is the paycheck; the intangible rewards are satisfaction and praise. In most families, the children only get praise. They have little opportunity to receive a paycheck, and little opportunity to have the satisfaction of a job well done. You don't need to salary up a five-year-old with $20 a week! A small reward, compensation for work, can make a huge difference for a young person.

The above is just a brief sketch to make clear that some of the terminology that is used in the business community is in fact more about human nature than about corporate workers. It is who we are. And once we realize that, we can take advantage of it. We are not imposing "business jargon" or "workforce ideas" on our children. We are allowing them to bloom in ways they are already designed and want to bloom.

In the next chapter, we will quickly tackle a few things that might get in the way of implementing this system. There are a few roadblocks that need to be removed, a few hurdles that need to be jumped. We need to deal with some misconceptions that arise. From there, we're going straight to the *My Millionaire Kids* game plan.

Chapter 2 Roadblocks

Our economy is in such bad shape it is obvious that we haven't been taught good money management. In the process of writing this book I realized that people have misconceptions about kids and money that are keeping them from handling money properly.

Some objections to this system arising from these misconceptions are:

1.   **"I don't want my child to think he will get paid for everything."**

This did not even come up with my children, but if a child is asked to do something and he says, "How much are you going to pay me?" Your response is, "You get paid to do the things in your Job Description. Everything else you do because it needs to be done. In every business, people have to do things for which they don't get paid. Someone has to make the coffee, help others when they get behind or do other tasks that their Supervisor asks them to do."

As it is now, your child is getting the idea that he won't get paid for anything. This sets up some wrong thinking. He might get the idea that his time and talents aren't worth anything, this can lead to the subconscious thought that he isn't worth anything.

There will be some special tasks, such as Spring Cleaning, that you might want to offer a Bonus.

2. **"I don't want my child to be greedy."** The cure for this is Giving. I had my children give away 10 %. We watched a TV show that cared for poor children around the world. I would add money to theirs and we would send a check once a month. They even wrote a letter and the host read it on the air!!!

Here is a note from my 22 year old son, Matthew

> *"When my sister and I were about 8 and 5 we had saved up $1000 (I forget how much exactly) and had decided to give it to a charity we wanted to help and we enclosed a letter with our ideas of how to help and spend the money. I still remember to this day having my mom and dad wake us up one morning so we could watch the show and hearing the letter we had written together. I was so excited that I knew that what I had done was important to someone in such a recognizable position. Looking back the ideas for the money were grandiose and impractical but no one told us because it didn't matter what was important to us was that grown ups used what we had done and appreciated it. "*

Dear James I think you should [...]
garden in rawanda for food [...]
and teach them how [...]
the food is ripe and how [...] plant [...] the [...]
depth and it will keep them [...]
pull weeds plant seeds and [...] the fruit of
their labor plus less of the [...]
that means more money for [...]
bowls spoons cloths beads [...]
for milk to make cheese fresh meat leather to
make bags and leather rope to plow fields to
pull out stumps of trees and the [...] to plow
out a war and extra money to buy chickens
for meat and eggs and the kids will learn
discipline and how to work hard at
caring for the chickens goats and their
fruits and vegetables they grow

Love Matthew and Milena
      age 10   age 7

PS Money is enclosed   hope you
get it soon and finish orphanage first
I'm glad yours doing what you can
do for them right now James don't
send us a Brick put the money to the
children in rawanda I will donate seeds for
garden if you decide to plant garden in Rawa

I think Matthew was 10 and I think the amount was $70. Dad
and I may or may not have added to it. But you see, a
memory doesn't have to be accurate for its effect to be life-
changing. We talk about "self-esteem" and try to give it to our

children in words of encouragement. Life events are so much more powerful. Hearing his letter read on the air was a defining moment in Matthew's life.

The charity my children chose for their giving also helped in developing their respect for property. My daughter always took very good care of her clothing because she said, "I want to give it to the poor children." When I was teaching her to sew, we made little sundresses to send to Africa, which gave an added element of pleasure and excitement to what could have been a boring lesson.

If your child does not respect his $1.00 socks, he is not going to respect your $20,000 car, just because you invested so much money in it. You cannot expect him to handle property responsibly when he turns 18 just because the property is expensive. This is a character issue that has to be taught and nurtured. It is not a mathematical issue.

3.   **"My child is going to be working his entire life. I just want him to enjoy his childhood."** For the reasons stated above, work is enjoyable. You are setting him up to have poor work habits and skills if you do not teach him the pleasure of a job well done. The consequence is that he will spend the rest of his life being miserable at work.

When you give your child chores and teach him to do them well, your are giving him hope. We think of hope as something in the future. Something you long for and want to happen; but hope actually begins in the past. I have hope for the future because of my experience in the past. I have hope that I will get paid on Friday, because my employer paid me every previous Friday.

There is a little voice in our heads that is programmed by experience. It says, "If I can make the bed, if I can mow the lawn, then I can accomplish this new task I am facing." That voice can go in the opposite direction, however. It can say, "If I failed at this, then I will fail at that; if I can't do this, I can't do that."

We have tried to give our children hope and encouragement by words; but we need to give them hope and encouragement by creating experiences in which they succeed. We say, 'You can do anything you want to do", or "You can do anything you set your mind to." This is incorrect. I do not have the natural ability to be an opera singer or a basketball player. It is much better to give them skills and challenges so that they discover what they really can do.

4.   "I am already giving him an allowance and he has chores, what's the difference?"

The My Millionaire Kids system gives you more bang for your buck, pardon the pun. It is more a matter of attitude than activity. You are giving him a vision for the future, a better reason for doing the work and an incentive that this benefits him.

A.   You are consciously preparing your child for the work world, not just getting the chores done.

B.   You are giving him more responsibility and control over his life. Under your guidance, he manages his own money. Most parents do not monitor how a child spends his allowance, except to prohibit certain things. Saving and investing are not taught in most homes

C.   You are helping him to discover his interests and talents to prepare for a life-long career that he will enjoy and do well.

D.   You are reducing the tension in the home.

When Ed and I were in training to become foster parents, the instructors told us that a research team had done a study asking people, "What was the worst thing you remember growing up?" The overwhelming answer was, "Yelling."

When the chores and allowance are directly connected, you don't have to yell, to get them to do what they need to do. If they refuse to work, you simply don't pay them. Make sure that there is a rule of no borrowing, and no paying a sibling to do your share without parental approval.

If the child is willing to go without money, he will not do his chores for a while. But eventually there will be something that he really wants and cannot afford. Make sure that you do not bail him out, no matter how much he cries and whines.

If a child still won't work then start revoking privileges.

5.   "Why would I pay my child to brush his teeth?"

When a child is very young his job is to take care of himself and his possessions." He is at an entry level position in The Family Business. You are teaching him to be responsible, thorough and dependable.

Also, in the beginning of your business, you must concentrate on the areas in your family that are causing tension.

> About what are you yelling?
>
> When are you using punishments?
>
> Do you have to tell them 6 times to go to bed?
>
> Do they go to school without brushing their teeth?
>
> Put these items on the Task Schedule first and see how the tension is reduced.

It might seem that you are rewarding him for bad behavior; but it doesn't work that way. Remember, the premise for starting a business is to see a need and then figure out a way to meet that need and get paid for it. It won't even enter into his head to think, "Hey, this is a good racket, what else can I mess up so that Mom and Dad will pay me for it?" Instead you will be helping him to develop the vision to see needs and the creative ability to meet the needs.

You need a child to pick up his things. You have tried all the explaining, punishing and other methods and still find his toys in the middle of the room. Try this, "Max, when we go to the hotel on vacation, the workers there keep the lobby and rooms nice and neat so we can enjoy ourselves. We need to keep our things nice and neat so that when people come over they can enjoy themselves. So, I am going to put on your Task Schedule that you are in charge of Maintenance for the Living Room. Let's make up a list of the things that need to be done."

You get his stuff (and yours) picked up in the living room and he gets better prepared for the business world. It's a win-win situation. He is not "doing chores," he is starting his Janitorial Service, and you are his first customer.

6.   "I have a "Treasure Chest", sticker book, special treat, etc." These are all great. If your budget allows, by paying your children and teaching them to manage the money, you are better preparing them for adulthood.

7.   "There are more important things than money."

Ask yourself the following: "Where did I get the idea that teaching my child how to properly manage money will make him morally corrupt and materialistic? Where did I get the idea that talking about money makes me a person who is "not nice."

When there is a need or tragedy, we are asked to give. The better we manage our money, the more we have to give.

The number one cause of divorce is money problems. Do you want to do something to reduce the chance of divorce in your child's life?

Poor people can be morally corrupt and materialistic. Poor people can get divorced.

Money touches every area of our lives. To ignore it, to ignore teaching our kids about it is irresponsible and setting them up for suffering and failure.

Teaching our kids about money, does not interfere with teaching them our moral values and principles. NOT teaching our kids about money will interfere with their ability to live out their moral principles and values.

The discipline and self-control of handling money enabled my children to demonstrate discipline and self-control in relationships, career, health and money management.

I want to strongly emphasize this: My children are moral, kind, generous and giving. They give of their time, talents, hearts and money to others. Their peers look up to them as someone who can encourage them and someone they want to emulate. I believe that they are morally strong because they are financially strong. The self-control "muscles" they developed from childhood are helping them to be self-controlled in all areas of their adult lives.

8.   "I just want my child to be happy."

Poor money management is probably one of the greatest sources of misery in this world. A person who has a passion for something that society has decided isn't worth a lot, will be able to fulfill his passion if he is a good money manager. Think of "starving artist." Many people have found happiness in working at a job that pays the bills just to fulfill their passion in their free time. An artist doesn't have to be "starving" if he has been managing his money from a young age. You have to be disciplined to achieve this.

If you are a poor money manager, are you happy? Would you be happier if you could straighten out your financial mess? Would you be immoral or greedy if you had more money?

9.   "We are in such bad financial shape (or I am such a bad housekeeper), how can I teach my kids what I don't know (or do)?"

There are two issues here, the doing and the reasoning. For the reasoning, say, "I didn't learn these things when I was your age, and I want to give you a better chance at success than I had, so we will learn together."

For the doing, just follow the very simple guidelines in this book and learn with your children. You are disciplined enough and smart enough to manage the money of an eight-year-old. You can do the housework that a ten-year-old can do. You may not be able to save 10% of your income, but you can save 10% of theirs. As these principles begin to work in your family, you will discover ways to improve your own financial situation and living conditions.

10.   "My kids already accept responsibility and are obedient."

That is great, but are you teaching them to manage money? My own story can tell what's missing here.

I grew up in a farmhouse in Pennsylvania. My father owned a small manufacturing facility and my mother stayed home. We had chores and got an allowance. We also got $1 for every A on our report card, which went into a savings account. I was an obedient child and a good student. I was able to memorize facts, ace the test and forget what I learned the next month. I pulled all-nighters to do my term papers. I had no discipline. We did our chores, but we hated them. We never saw ourselves as part of the Family Business. We never got the idea that we were being prepared for success.

My parents instilled many wonderful and important values in us. I owe my successes in life more to them than to anyone else. BUT, my parents never taught us to manage money. When I graduated from college, I floundered. I was always broke. I worked hard and made enough money, but wasted it. I never found a career that inspired my passion.

I married an engineer who also was never taught to manage money. We spent the first 20 years of our marriage wasting his income. He worked hard and we didn't go into debt but we didn't save or invest like we should have.

Now, we understand how to manage money, and have made more progress in the last 5 years, than in the first 20. It is never too late to get your life on track.

But, our children are more disciplined <u>in every area</u> than we are. I believe that teaching them to manage money in addition to teaching them to be responsible, obedient, hard-working, generous and disciplined has made the difference.

It is not what only you earn that determines your success, it is how well you manage it. The money we **wasted** is what we should have saved and invested.

11. I want my children to concentrate on education and only those things that will get them into prestigious colleges and allow them to become professionals. I don't care whether or not they do chores.

This mindset is pervasive in our culture and it has done much damage, to people and to our society.

I remember many conversations with other parents while formulating the MMK System. Sometimes they would argue that since their children were going to be doctors or lawyers, they did not need to take up the menial tasks of housework. Instead, they insisted, their children would only concentrate on academic achievement and extra-curricular activities. There is mistaken understanding of what it means to be a truly successful person.

Your child may become a lawyer and hire a landscaper, but doing yard work will make him a better lawyer. Because doing yard work will make your child understand that in families we don't only do the things we want to do or even the things we do especially well. In families, we are a team and teamwork means doing whatever is necessary for the team to achieve its goals. Obviously this is the basic building block of the idea of community and communities are the basic units composing a society.

Commentators are often lamenting the lack of community in America. Everyone lives behind walls. Either the walls of a gated housing development or the walls of privilege or the walls of our jobs which we allow to define us. Is it any wonder we have become so fragmented as a society?

Also, all jobs share the elements of organization, discipline, time management, thoroughness, coordination and many other qualities. Doing any job makes your more prepared for success.

Teaching children at a very young age that the most important thing in life is to achieve success in school so as to achieve success in a vocation is a recipe for disaster. Your child may become a skilled doctor, but what preparation has he or she had for being a good father or mother? For being a good community member or a good citizen? Furthermore, when your entire sense of self-worth is tied into a single area, you are in a very vulnerable position.

We want children who are integrated and who attain success on every human level, in particular relationships. And yes, this has a lot to do with yard work and other household tasks-and yes, it is a lesson that must be taught early and often.

12.   I am already preparing my child for success.

Consider these statistics:

> Out of 100 people who start working at the age of 25, by the age 65:
>
> * 1% are wealthy
>
> * 4% have adequate capital stowed away for retirement
>
> * 3% are still working
>
> * 63% are dependant on Social Security, friends, relatives or charity.
>
> * 29% are dead.

To my astonishment, these were the same numbers I was taught in high school, and I did nothing to put myself in the 5%. In the last 50 years, nothing has changed. We are not doing what it takes to put our children in the 5%.

My Millionaire Kids, is the only system proven to put children in the 5% category no matter what their income level, passion, job or career choice or educational opportunities.

With these roadblocks removed, let's get right to the *My Millionaire Kids System*.

Chapter 3 Getting Started – When

Many organizations are recognizing that our young people are poorly prepared for life on their own. Most of them are preparing curricula and programs to be taught at the high school level. This is too late. The habits and attitudes that stay with us for a life time begin long before elementary school

 I introduced my daughter to an early version of the *My Millionaire Kids System*, when she was only 3. Now at 19 she is doing very well. By using the *My Millionaire Kids System* (hereafter **MMK System**) business model, we are giving our children tools they can use at home and in the workplace.

Everyone can see from the world of nature, that a seed planted sooner yields sooner and over time yields more fruit, than a seed planted later. If we teach our children organization, creativity, discipline and many other things at a young age, their "seeds" will produce much more fruit. In using these tools from a young age, just like any muscle, our children are developing internal strength to use these tools under pressure. Isn't that the working definition of "accepting responsibility" - being moved to take action based on internal not external pressure?

Several years ago I watched a show on public television featuring recent developments in brain science. One scientist used computer-generated brains to illustrate brain development. He said that children learn by <u>doing</u> not <u>lecturing</u> and he showed the connections and pathways that were developed when engaged in various tasks. Each task your child does creates brain pathways that will multiply, develop and strengthen to make your child stronger and smarter in later life. The pathways developed at an early age have more time to be reinforced and become strong.

Also, we have charts that show the benefit of saving a small amount of money from an early age. Parents, this is not some hypothetical chart in a book, this is my daughter's actual investment status as of December 31, 2009.

The best time for your children to invest is before they have a mortgage, car payment and kids. Even if they can't add to their investment every year, it will still grow and be a nice sum at retirement.

My son stayed at home and put himself through a local college because he realized that cash was more important to him than a degree from an expensive school. Instead of getting a full time job, he worked 3 part time jobs so he could have a flexible schedule. He wanted to be available to continue the volunteer work he was doing and the only way to do that was to have part time jobs.

They both bought used cars which saved a car payment and comprehensive insurance cost.

Milena has $9,800.00 invested in her self-directed ROTH IRA now. She is currently earning 17% in a residential real estate rental. If she continues to contribute the maximum amount of $5,000 and continues to earn 17% she will have over $53,000,000.00 at retirement -- TAX FREE.

If she only earns 10% but continues to contribute $5,000.00 then she will have over $4,000,000.00 at retirement. If she has an emergency, wants to buy a house or pay for college, she can take out the money she put in without penalty, but will have less money growing for the future.

	Interest Rate	17%	Interest Rate	10%
	Annual Contribution	$ 5,000.00	Annual Contribution	$ 5,000.00
Initial Amt	$ 9,800.00	Age 19	$ 9,800.00	Age 19
Year 2	$ 16,642.81	Age 20	$ 16,642.81	Age 20
Year 3	$ 24,472.09	Age 21	$ 23,307.09	Age 21
Year 4	$ 33,632.34	Age 22	$ 30,637.80	Age 22
Year 5	$ 44,349.84	Age 23	$ 38,701.58	Age 23
Year 20	$ 747,941.25	Age 38	$ 320,528.51	Age 38
Year 21	$ 880,091.26	Age 39	$ 357,581.36	Age 39
Year 22	**$ 1,034,706.78**	**Age 40**	**$ 398,339.50**	Age 40
Year 23	$ 1,215,606.93	Age 41	$ 443,173.45	Age 41
Year 30	$ 3,707,190.78	Age 48	$ 911,055.54	Age 48
Year 31	$ 4,342,413.21	Age 49	$ 1,007,161.09	Age 49
Year 38	$ 3,091,493.48	Age 56	$ 2,010,107.90	Age 56
Year 39	$ 5,322,047.37	Age 57	$ 2,216,118.68	Age 57
Year 40	$ 17,931,795.42	Age 58	$ 2,442,730.55	Age 58
Year 41	$ 20,985,200.64	Age 59	$ 2,692,003.61	Age 59
Year 42	$ 24,557,684.75	Age 60	$ 2,966,203.97	Age 60
Year 43	$ 28,737,491.16	Age 61	$ 3,267,824.37	Age 61
Year 44	$ 33,627,864.65	Age 62	$ 3,599,606.80	Age 62
Year 45	$ 39,349,601.64	Age 63	$ 3,964,567.48	Age 63
Year 46	$ 46,044,033.92	Age 64	$ 4,366,024.23	Age 64
Year 47	$ 53,876,519.69	Age 65	$ 4,807,626.66	Age 65

Every business has a goal, or Product. Some businesses create things such as cars and clothing. Other businesses provide a service such as lawn maintenance or dry cleaning. In the process of producing the product, the Business has to have enough money to feed its people (Wages). The goal of

The Family Business is to produce happy, healthy, well-adjusted productive adults and to feed them along the way.

Get started NOW. No matter what age your child is, or if you have several children of different ages, the business is run the same way. You do not have to have a different system for each age. The Jobs will be different based on age and skill, just as in the Workplace, each person's job is based on his experience, skill, seniority, etc. But each Employee has the same basics: Come to work, do your Job, collect Wages or Salary, Go Home and have fun with the money you made and the people you love

Your home is already running on some sort of system. The extent to which you have defined and communicated that system will dictate how much each family member (Employee) understands and does his part (Job).

Everyone has worked in companies that had poor Management. No matter how skilled or determined a worker may be, poor management leads to misery. By instituting the Effective Business Practices of the **MMK System**, you are not only creating a happy home, but preparing your children to understand and be effective in the work world.

During the production process, we all would like to work in an environment that is pleasant. In a poorly managed business, there are people who don't understand the system of the business and how they fit in. They may wander from desk to desk distracting and irritating their hard-working Co-Workers. This creates tension and an unpleasant environment.

In the same way, a child of any age who does not understand, or has never been taught the goals and principles of The Family Business becomes a distraction. While Mom is cooking supper, he is constantly interrupting, because he wants to Belong and Contribute. Telling him to watch TV until dinner is ready will either defeat his spirit or cause him to escalate his bad behavior.

Is it ever too early for a child to feel he belongs; to feel like his work is important to the family. Is he ever too young to know the fulfillment of being part of a team?

The answer is obvious. So let's get started.

CHAPTER 4 Getting Started – HOW

Setting up a business is more complex than setting up the family business based on the **MMK System**. I am using the business format because it prepares your child for the "real" world. These exercises are all you need to set up Your Family Business. Don't be deceived into thinking "It can't be that simple." Instead tell yourself, "This is so simple I simply <u>must</u> give it a try and I'll start right away!"

1.   Do an Assessment

When a person starts a business, he identifies a need, or problem and then goes about meeting that need. If people are hungry, you want to start a farm or open a grocery store. Then you determine the steps to accomplish that Goal.

Each parent has several areas in which his child is not accepting responsibility, "Doing his Job." This is a problem that requires a solution. For one mom, it's getting her child to keep his soccer equipment organized, for another it is cooperation doing chores, and another just wants to leave the house with everything needed and without World War III.

The first step is to step back. Find a few hours when you can be quiet and alone. Get your spouse to do the same. Engage in this separately and then come together to compare notes. You will probably have noticed a few things that your spouse has not and vice versa.

During this time you determine your needs and problems. What is frustrating you? What are your children doing or not doing that worries you? What do you wish for in your family? What do you want to go away.

Ask yourself, "what am I yelling about?"

2. Make a Business Plan

After determining your needs for each child, fill out a spread sheet on the computer, or lined paper. Write in 10 tasks for 5 days a week. If there is a task that is not done daily, such as Dusting, then put another task in that slot for the other days, such as Vacuuming.

When you really consider all the work that needs to get done around your house, you will quickly realize there are more than 10 tasks for an Employee or Family Member. Once you locate the first ten, you'll discover many others. I never got past the first 10 because my children became responsible, self-controlled, disciplined and their tasks just expanded.

Decide how much you will pay your child. For very young children, a nickel or dime is sufficient. The amount of money isn't as important as the fact that they are being Paid (rewarded) for their efforts. If a child is older, the compensation can start out small, only symbolic, and be adjusted as he improves his Skill. At some point you will have to decide the Wages based on the difficulty of the task and your family's income level. And, if they start earning money outside the home, then you will either not increase their Wages, or discontinue it.

Many families already have Chore Charts and reward systems that are working pretty well. I would only suggest that you start using Business Terminology for what you are doing and expand the Business Model to other areas of your family life. This will better prepare your child for success in the work world.

You may even make up one for the Parents (Executives). In the Work world, the Business Owner or Executives make the Management decisions with varying degrees of Employee input. You have to decide what level of input your child will have in setting up The Family Business, based on age and other family dynamics already in place.

3.   Set up your Office

a.   You will need an Job Description and Schedule (Chore Chart) for each child (Staff). You will need a Schedule for every week. The Supervisor checks off each successfully completed task.

b.   Each Employee will need an Accounting page. You can use a plain piece of ruled paper and just draw columns on it with a ruler. You can purchase the green ledger sheets, or you can use a computer accounting system, or join the My Millionaire Kids Network and we provide all the tools you need. Remember, you are trying to make everything "official." Children respond to that. It makes them feel grown up. If it's just a sheet of paper on the refrigerator that was hastily put together, they will be less inspired. The little things count in the **MMK System**.

c.   You will need to make up a Training Manual. When we were growing up, most of our parents said, "go clean your room." And they never told us how to do it properly, efficiently and thoroughly. By taking time to teach your child how to do the various tasks, you are investing those tasks with importance. You are sharing your wisdom and your time and this alone speaks volumes to a child.

The easiest thing is to do the task yourself and make notes. Then transfer these notes to 3 x 5 cards or papers that can be taped to the wall until the child is doing the task well. Each one of these is the Job Description. All the Job Descriptions together make the Training Manual.

For example, making the bed. Go into your room and make the bed with the child. Make it fun, explaining along the way. "Put on the fitted bottom sheet." "Put on the top sheet". "Put on the blanket," etc. Your child will see the tasks not as orders to be fulfilled, but as significant endeavors that you have considered and prepared for him.

When you Train the child to make the bed, you will demonstrate the easiest, quickest and proper way to do each step. The Training Manual converts vague commands into something tangible. The Employee can look at the card to make sure he has done each step. The Supervisor will do the task with the child until he can do it correctly on his own. Then the Supervisor will make periodic Quality Control checks.

We have all the tools and training videos in the My Millionaire Kids Network. So even if you can't cook, your child can.

## 4.	Have a Staff Meeting.

If your children are small, you can simply tell them how proud you are that they have been helping and now they are going to be paid and share in The Family Business.

If your children have been uncooperative in some areas, tell them that grown ups get paid to do their jobs, and that you are going to pay them to do these specific tasks. Be prepared to see how quickly your disciplinary problems vanish.

If your children are older, you can tell them that you are setting up The Family Business in order to better prepare them to succeed in the work world.

5.   Get Started

Pick a day, and get started.   Analyze as you go and make adjustments. You may want to do a dry run on the weekend and start keeping records on Monday. If you hit a snag, e-mail us, the System works, don't give up.

6.   Pay Day.

For very small children, you may want to get a stack of dimes and pay them for each task, or each day. Very young children would rather have 10 dimes than 1 dollar because, "10 is more than 1" and dimes are shiny and pretty.

If your family budget is strained, you can use a point system. You are already spending on your children unless they are running around naked. In this case, stop buying necessities such as clothing. When a child needs new shoes, take her to the store, tell her how much money she has "earned." If she has earned enough for the shoes, she can pick them out (with your guidance as to quality, usefulness, durability, etc., Cost/Benefit Ratio). If she has not earned enough, or if you want to Partner with her, you can say, "you have earned $5.00 so if you pay 1/2 for the shoes, I will pay 1/2. If she finds a pair on sale for $6.00, you both save.

You can also have a "store" in your house. If you have purchased items, assign them a point value and allow your child to shop. This is similar to the "treasure box" concept.

Be prepared to be surprised again at how quickly your child becomes a smart shopper. You will laugh at yourself when you realize how much money you wasted when they were spending your money.

If you are wealthy and have hired people to clean your house and do yard-work, it is even more important for you to train your child in The Family Business. At some point you hope to transfer this wealth to him and you certainly don't want him to squander it or ruin his life with it. Statistics show that inherited wealth and inherited businesses are lost in the second or third generation. Again, if you do not teach your child good money management, many of you will be heartbroken when he squanders your wealth or ruins his life.

Think about 10 things that you are paying someone to do, and transfer them to your child. You can pay him a nominal sum, or you can pay him the same amount you are paying the Employee. You can begin now to transfer wealth to him and there are great tax advantages to doing so. Ask your accountant.

There is nothing better than On-The-Job Training. Nothing better than starting early. Nothing better than training your child the way you want him to be trained. Nothing better than giving him a leg up and a head start in life.

That is what the MMK System is all about.

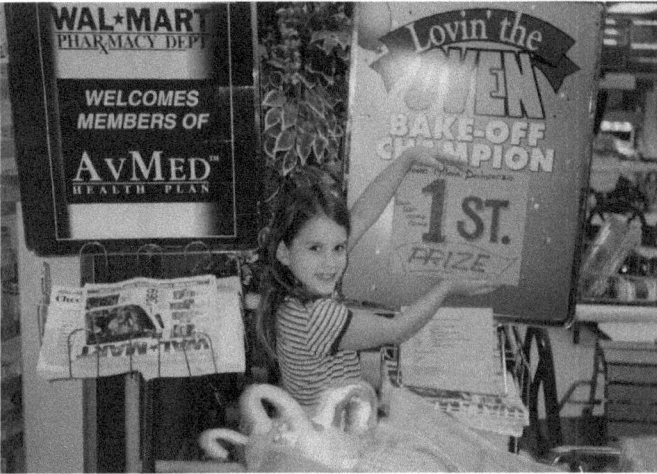

Milena was thrilled when she won First Place in the
Christmas cookie contest.

The next year she won first place again and
Matthew second.

It didn't dampen their enthusiasm one bit when they
found out- *they were the only contestants!*

Daddy's birthday - Lemon Cheesecake

They learned to cook by making fun desserts- but by the time they were 12 they could make dinner. One evening I was chatting with a friend, and didn't come home until ½ hour after dinner. When I walked in dinner was on the table- not peanut butter and jelly sandwiches, but the meal I had planned

As long as there are trees, you can entertain kids for free. The fun is doubled with kids from the neighborhood.

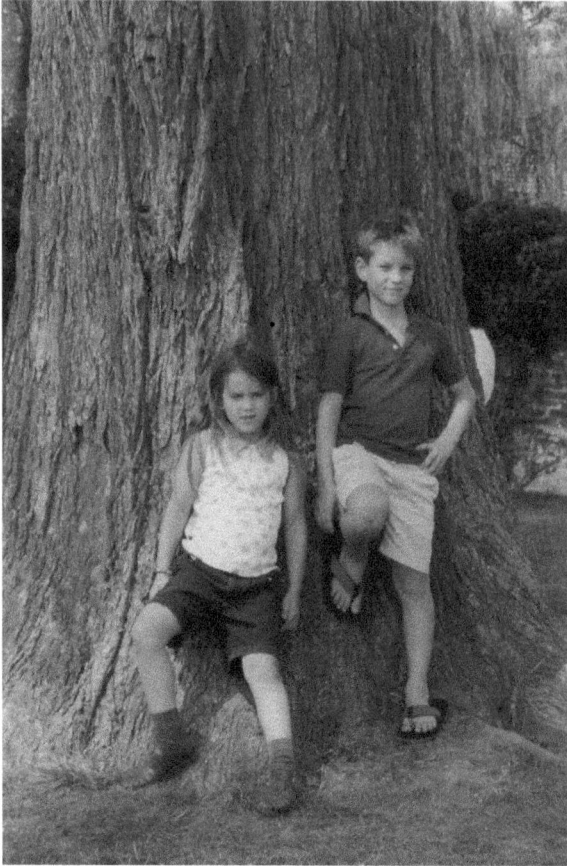

The Original My Millionaire Kids

Chapter 5

You said What? Things kids hate to hear

We already said that the thing kids hate most is yelling. Here are some comments that we have repeated so much they have become part of the fabric of family life. The circumstances prompting these comments must be widespread.

Money doesn't grow on trees. and You have champagne taste on a beer budget.

Why did we say that? Our child has just asked for something beyond the range of our budget, is frivolous or he has just ruined something.

In the case of asking for something that is expensive or frivolous - we do a Cost/Benefit Analysis. Yes, use that big phrase, even on a 3-year-old.

When we were at Disney's Animal Kingdom, my daughter wanted an animal-shaped back pack. I said, "It costs $12 and you have $20. If you buy it, you will have $8 left over." The disgust on her face was hysterical as she said, "It's not worth it."

Your child lost his clothes at gym class, a sleep-over or wore her dress shoes to the playground. You pleasantly say, "We have to go to the store and buy new _____. Let's look at your Accounting Sheet and see how much money you have. "

Depending on how much money he has, how responsible he has been and how old he is, you make a decision as to what share he will have in the purchase. For example, you could say, "Ok, you have $20. The jeans will be $10. I will pay half and you pay half and you will have $15 left over." If this has happened several times and the child isn't getting the message, increase his percentage. It isn't all bad. Shopping is fun so he will get some enjoyment out of his consequences.

Close the door, were you born in a barn?

Years ago a financial guru wrote in the newspaper, that no matter what our income, we all waste 10%. Just think, that 10% could fund our retirement. We have to admit that parents are bad at this, but we can learn right along with the kids and mend our ways.

When you sit down to pay the bills, compare each month's usage, and the cost difference. Let's say that the electric bill last month was $100.00. Now, say this, "OK, we are going to do a scientific experiment. We are going to time our showers to 3 minutes. We are going to put a list of leftovers on the outside of the fridge so we know what our choices are before we open the door and we are going to hang a bell on the door knob to remind us to make sure the door is completely shut. Now, everyone guess how much money we will save and put it on a piece of paper. The next month, if we have saved any money, the person who guesses closest gets half the money and the rest is used for family expenses."

In the case of wasted food, kids will eat a larger variety of foods if they have an hand in preparation. Also, don't push their taste buds too fast. Ask them to take 1 bite of a new food, and wash it down with 1 bite of a food they like. If you treat them like intelligent, self-controlled human beings they will be more willing.

OH NO, you _____

It's the distressed OH NO, that hurts the child. "You lost your _____, you ruined _____, you broke _____." Don't beat yourself up for having spontaneous emotions. An occasional outburst proves you are human, especially if you are surprised by the discovery. But these will be kept to a minimum if you know how to handle these situations.

If the kids were running and roughhousing inside and broke a lamp, if they lost something or ruined something, you negotiate the finances as described earlier.

We Can't Afford It

Unless we tell them, kids don't know where we get our money. They do not know that you can work a whole week and spend it in an hour at the grocery store. They do not know how hard work is, even work we like.

Our children are going to have to work and they need to manage the fruits of their work well so they can enjoy life more.

Instead of "We can't afford it." Do a Cost/Benefit Analysis. Give them the opportunity to decide what they are willing to give up in order to have something else. Give them the opportunity to think of ideas to increase their income.

What is so powerful about this is that you are no longer playing the role of Ebenezer Scrooge who dictatorially denies your children things they want for mysterious reasons. In the MMK system, you bring your child into the decision-making process. "So, you want the top-of-the-line bicycle? Well, I can understand why. It's beautiful and it's very well made. It's more than we have budgeted so let's take a look at the numbers and see what we can do."

Suddenly, you're on the same team trying to make limited resources work. You want your child to have the bicycle and together you two can figure out a way to make it work - he may have to wait another six months to get the bike and do more work around the house - or he may realize the cost of the bike is more than he wants to pay. Either way, you are on your child's team, wishing the very best for your child. In other words, you are a family.

I don't have time

Your child asks to go to the beach on Saturday. You have too much laundry and cleaning to do, so you either say no, or you go and are not much fun because you are thinking about all the undone work left at home.

Instead, you can say, "I would love to spend that time with you on Saturday, but I have too much housework to do that day. Let's see what Jobs you can do for me so that we have the extra time to go to the beach. What can we get done weeknights instead of waiting till Saturday?"

When I was growing up, a friend's family had cleaning night on Thursday so that they had the weekend free. Every member of the family had assigned tasks and they went through that house like greased lightning.

If you consistently apply the MMK System, it won't be long before your home is operating like a well-run factory, and one of the greatest benefits the family will get is time: more time, time without stress and worry.

Chapter 6

Find and Use Educational Opportunities

When it comes to learning, children are sponges. Without any effort, they can learn two languages before they go to kindergarten. They think everything is fun and interesting. We have to teach them bad attitudes. We have to shuffle them off into computer addiction. Teach your child everything you know, read books together, let them participate in everything you do. You will be surprised that, after you have let her help organize the spices, she might find a better way to do it.

While you are cooking, go over math skills, talk about chemistry, and nutrition. Give them everything you know about why you eat what you eat.

But what if there are important things that you don't really know much about? If you have a bad diet and you don't know much about food or nutrition, this can be an excellent opportunity for you and your children to learn together. If you tackle some area of ignorance with tenacity and excitement and let your children in on the process, that will do more to ensure the success of your children than any lecture could ever do.

Learn the simplest of money management. Earn, save 10%, give 10% and spend the rest wisely. Even if you can't do that, they can.

If the whole house is in chaos, start by concentrating on each child's room (Workspace). Figure out, room by room, what are the problems. View the disorganized room as a need to be met. Go into the room and make a study of it with your child. With pen and paper itemize what's wrong, and teach him organizational principles. Before you know it, your child - the one who had been making the mess - will be leaping to identify why things are messy; how they got messy; and how to remedy it.

Once it is organized, they will be better at keeping it organized than you are.

Don't feel guilty. Most of us had a haphazard upbringing when it comes to life skills. It's an epidemic. We are who we are. But we can give our kids a better chance than we had. Our parents did their best, now we can do our best. You may not have had a good education - but you can read a first or second grade book. By doing things with your child, you will become a better person.

Apprenticeship

Some of my fondest memories are the times when my brothers and I spent a Saturday riding with the local veterinarian. I can still hear the squeal of baby pigs as we held them to be vaccinated and feel the rush of chasing calves. At one time I wanted to be a vet, but was discouraged because I was "a girl."

There are dozens of small business owners that you know who would be more than happy to spend time with your children. Most of them love what they do, love to talk about it, love to teach it and want the business to carry on after they retire. Instead of having your child spend Saturday morning playing video games while you try to do all the housework, have him spend the morning helping you, and then let him spend his afternoon with an entrepreneur.

At first, this would be voluntary, But if your child has any discipline and willingness to work, most of these businesses can find something he can do for a small wage.

You might think, "If I pay a child to work around my house, aren't I taking money away from a businessman that is trying to feed his family?" No, there are so many jobs that are too small for a business to even consider. They have overhead, equipment, labor costs, etc. which make small jobs unprofitable.

You are actually helping them on two fronts:

1.   You are doing the small jobs that they don't want

2.   You are giving a child on-the-job training, which saves the business owner money when he hires that child, at the time he enters the workforce. By reducing or eliminating the business owner's training cost, you have made yourself a better employee, and that might even make the difference of even being chosen over the other candidates applying for the job.

Eventually your child will discover a career choice based on actual knowledge and experience and you can narrow his focus to develop the skills he needs in that choice. Even if he is bound for college, this will be of great benefit. My son has a degree in Civil Engineering/Construction Management. All the building and remodeling we did gave him a love for construction, as well as skills and made it easier to understand the underlying geometry, physics and math.

Chapter 7 Doped up on Dopamine

Dopamine is a chemical that is secreted in our brains when we experience something that pleases us - a roller coaster ride, winning a game, receiving a smile. The problem is that the more we are stimulated, the more we need to feel pleasure. In common terms "the more it takes to make us happy."

Our children are over stimulated. Everything has to be exciting, fun, loud, expensive. Nothing can be quiet and simple. Do not expose your child to artificial entertainment at an early age. Limit TV, severely limit the computer and video games. Take them for walks. They love to pick up rocks and sticks. Let them have a collection. Play board games. Plant a tomato or a whole garden.

Things don't have to be fun - like cleaning - but they don't have to be unpleasant - and some things are necessary. Washing dishes is not fun, but doing it together gives you the chance to talk - that makes it pleasant.

Our children need a thrill, they need excitement. That's why they do crazy things like jump off high places, ride their bikes as fast as they can and take other chances. You can give them the thrill of accomplishment, of having their own money to manage and tackling a new skill. When they have these things in their lives, they are less likely to experiment with risky behavior. There are few things on this earth that are more daring, thrilling and challenging than starting your own business - and more rewarding.

We never know what life is going to hand us. We may be wealthy - but a hurricane can turn our life upside down. Learning to make the best of the good and the bad will keep us from being miserable. The more skills we have, the easier and more quickly we can turn around adverse circumstances.

Children think that the MMK System is FUN. That's the beauty of Systems. They give us more than we bargain for. Don't try to analyze or understand it. They think they're having fun and that's all that counts.

Words of Advice

Moms - toughen up. You can't buy your child everything he wants. You can't fix everything - sometimes it's better to let them suffer the consequences of a bad decision and sometimes they have to cry. They are going to leave home, so they are better off if you start training them to be independent early. But be prepared for the pain. At some point I said to a friend, "I raised my kids to be independent, but

I didn't raise them to be independent from me!" My independent daughter drops by a few evenings a week to update me on her life and even ask for advice. My independent son calls regularly to discuss his life.

You can't build their self-esteem or hope by praising them when they don't deserve it. You don't have to beat them up with criticism, but to tell a child who did a poor job, that he did well is cheating him of learning excellence.

Dads - get involved. It is not enough to bring home the bacon. If you want your children to see you as a person and not a paycheck - participate. So what if it takes you twice as long to mow the lawn because your 6-year-old want to "help." So what if you miss the first half of the football game.

Parents - lighten up. It doesn't matter how inadequate you feel. Your child doesn't have a score sheet. You are capable of doing what a 3-year-old can do. Do it with him and he will be thrilled. Grow together. Also, even if you do the right things, you will do things that your child sees as wrong because he is a child. He won't realize that you made the right decisions until he is a parent.

Anyone can wash dishes, dust, hang up clothes, do a load of wash, take out the trash. Use the guidelines in this book to set it up like a business, do things together and watch. Be prepared to be surprised at how well you do at this parenting thing.

Chapter 8 Testimonials

Today my son is 24 and my daughter 21 and are successfully following their career paths. They are financially and morally strong. But more importantly, they are still a part of My Family. My daughter and I *and her friends*, are collaborating on a business and my son and I remodeled a house together. We have a great relationship. I am living every mother's dream, my kids and I have a healthy on-going relationship.

I hope that you will start today, and I can add your testimonial to the back of this book.

Quick Reference:

1. Write down the things that are causing tension in the home

2. Decide on 10 tasks for 5 days that will be each child's Job.

3. Decide on payment amounts

4. Fill out the Job Description and Task Schedule for each child.

5. Have a family meeting: explain the new Business and assign work

6. Teach each child the proper way to do his job

7. Start the system, do quality control and make adjustments

8. Pay Day, fill out Accounting Sheets

9. Analyze, improve, adjust

10. Enjoy!

Don't add stress to your life by trying to set up Your Family Business alone

Go To

MyMillionaireKids.com

Join the My Millionaire Kids Network, where we give you all the tools you need to"

- **Get Started**
- **Keep Going**
- **Be Successful**

You will receive:

- The Cooking By Calendar System
    - o Menu Calendar
    - o Cost - Cutting Inventory Sheet
    - o 30 Recipes Kids Can Cook
    - o How-to videos for cooking skills and preparing recipes
- Business Forms
    - o Task Schedules
    - o Accounting Ledger Sheets
    - o Employee Task Instructions
    - o Glossary of MMK Business Terms
- Instructional Videos
- Ongoing support by e-mail, forums and blogs

www.ingramcontent.com/pod-product-compliance
Lightning Source LLC
Chambersburg PA
CBHW060555100426
42742CB00013B/2570